HEADStart

GREAT CHIEFS

First published in Great Britain by
CAXTON EDITIONS
an imprint of
The Caxton Book Company,
16 Connaught Street,
Marble Arch, London, W2 2AF.

ISBN 1 84067 025 8

A copy of the CIP data for this book is available from the British Library upon request.

With grateful thanks to Helen Courtney

Created and produced for Caxton Editions by
FLAME TREE PUBLISHING,
a part of The Foundry Creative Media Company Ltd,
Crabtree Hall, Crabtree Lane,
Fulham, London, SW6 6TY.

Printed and bound in Singapore

HEADstart

GREAT CHIEFS

The History of the
Greatest Warriors Explained
in Glorious Colour

KAREN SULLIVAN

CAXTON EDITIONS

Contents

Who Were the First Americans?

In 1492, when Christopher Columbus landed at the Caribbean island of Hispaniola, he believed that he had reached the East Indies. As a result, he called the people who lived on the island 'Indians'. The name is still used today to refer to the native people of North, Central, and South America.

Some archaeologists believe that the first people trekked across into America during the Ice Age, nearly 12,000 years ago. Stone weapons, mainly arrowheads, have been found that date from over 10,000 years ago, proving that America was inhabited at this time. Other experts believe that the ancestors of the Native Americans entered the country from Asia more than 20,000 years ago.

Over the next 5,000 years, these people evolved from being hunters, who followed herds of large animals such as mammoths, to being farmers and craftsmen who lived in permanent settlements.

By the sixteenth century, Canada and the USA had become home to about 1.3 million people, who travelled across the continent and formed more than 300 tribes, speaking at least 200 different languages. The native North Americans were spread across ten different areas: arctic, subarctic, plains, plateau, great basin, north-west, California, south-west, south-east and north-east. These tribes changed constantly, as their members were forced to move when the animals they hunted became extinct, and because of drought and wars between the tribes.

The Life of the Native Americans

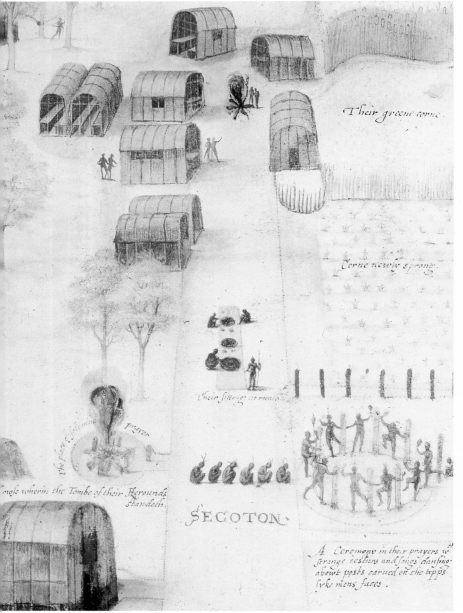

Their greene corne.

Corne newly sprong.

Their sitting at meate.

the place of solemne prayer.

A noise wherin the Tombe of their Herounds standeth.

SECOTON.

A Ceremony in their prayers wt strange tostures and songs dansinge about posts carved on the topps lyke mens faces.

Early American societies consisted of bands of 20 to 50 people, who lived by collecting wild plants and hunting animals for food. For shelter, the 'nomadic' people, those who moved around rather than staying in a permanent village, generally used small tepees, tents, or wigwams which were easy to pack up carry. Eventually they began to plant crops and by the time the Europeans arrived, maize, beans, squash and potatoes were being grown. Groups who grew crops generally lived in tribes of about 100 to 1,000 members. These tribes built relatively permanent villages. Feuds, raids, and wars often occurred between tribes.

Native Americans believed that the universe was controlled by supernatural forces. They thought that spirits lived in natural objects, such as rocks, trees and rivers, or in natural forces such as lightning. Good and evil spirits were believed to influence the outcome of hunts, fights, love, health and almost every aspect of everyday life. All Native American cultures had different methods of calling on these spirits to help them face life's unpredictable events. Cures for everything, from illnesses to poor farming, were provided by religious leaders – called shamans. The natives massaged, danced, sang and smoked tobacco with the aid of spirit helpers, to encourage the spirits to help them.

What Happened When the Europeans Arrived?

The first European people to discover the 'New World' of the Americas were the Spanish on a quest for gold and adventure. They often married the natives, creating a large, mixed class in Latin America, called 'mestizos'. In Canada, the first French explorers were mostly trappers and traders; they, too, often married the Indians, and they kept up friendly relations with each other.

However, the earliest English-Americans came to North America with their families in order to set up new settlements or 'colonies', and they tried to buy the land from the Native Americans. This caused many problems, because the Indians did not want to give up their homeland to the new settlers.

In about 1815, the US government decided that the Indians must leave their traditional territories and move to special areas that were run by the government. These were called 'reservations'. Between 1830 and 1840 more than 70,000 south-eastern peoples from many tribes were moved to the new Indian Territory in Oklahoma. This land already belonged to other Native Americans, and there was much fighting between the tribes.

By the mid-1800s, white settlers were travelling further west across the Great Plains. The Indians who lived on the Plains and in the Far West were often attacked and killed by groups of travellers. Many Indians also died from the diseases that the Europeans brought with them.

15

Indian Wars

The wars between the Native Americans and the Europeans began when the first white people arrived in 1540, and they continued for 350 years. Wars with the Indians were part of daily life, as the Europeans moved further across North America in search of land, gold and a new life.

As people from more and more countries in Europe arrived in America, they began to fight one another. Every country tried to use the Indians in their wars, and this caused a great deal of trouble between the different tribes, which were forced to take sides.

In the mid-nineteenth century the wars spread to the plains, mountains and deserts of the Western United States. When gold was discovered in California in 1848, the plan for the Indians to have their own frontier along the edge of the Great Plains was shattered. A series of bloody battles was the result, and many Indians and white settlers were massacred.

When the British arrived in America, they decided to set up 'treaties' with the Indians, which meant that the Indians and the new arrivals would agree terms peacefully about who should settle in certain areas, instead of just fighting over the territories. Soon the US government was also using the treaty system.

The white settlers nearly always managed to get the land they wanted, though. They would bribe the Indians with money, alcohol and promises of a new life in another area. The new settlers grew more and more greedy and in 1871 the use of treaties was abandoned by the US government, and it was decided that Indians would be ruled instead by the white people's laws. Many of the great chiefs from various tribes became known for their courage and skills in the Indian wars.

Hiawatha

Long one of the favourite characters of American folklore, Hiawatha was an American Indian who is best known as the hero of Henry Wadsworth Longfellow's poem, 'The Song of Hiawatha', which was published in 1855.

In Longfellow's poem, Hiawatha is a member of the Ojibwa tribe. Raised by his grandmother, Nokomis, Hiawatha is able to talk to the animals of the forest and surpasses all the other boys of his tribe in manly skills. He grows up to be a leader of his people, marries the Indian maiden Minnehaha, and acts as a peacemaker among warring tribes.

The real Hiawatha was a Mohawk Indian chief who lived in the late 1500s. His name means 'he who makes rivers'. Hiawatha was responsible for founding the 'Five Nations Iroquois League' at the request of the holy man Deganawidah. This League, which ended many of the wars that raged between Indians of the Iroquois tribes, had a sophisticated form of govern-ment, and some say that it became the model for the early US govern-ment. Tradition also credits him with introducing maize and fish oil to his people and with originating picture writing, new navigation techniques, and the practice of medicine.

Powhatan and the Legend of Pocahontas

Powhatan (1547–1618) was the chief of the 'Powhatan Confederacy', a group of more than 30 tribes, and the father of Pocahontas. At the time of the English settlement of Jamestown in 1607, the powerful Powhatan was friendly to the English. However, when he learnt that John Smith, the leader of the white settlement, was trying to find gold in the Indian lands, Powhatan decided to drive the settlers out.

When Smith was captured by the Indians, Powhatan left the Englishman's fate in the hands of his warriors, who were going to kill him. Pocahontas, Powhatan's favourite daughter, is said to have saved Smith's life, and probably the lives of everyone in the Jamestown colony. According to John Smith's book, called the *General Historie of Virginia,* he had been set before an altar stone to be killed, but was saved when Pocohontas threw herself over his body. Pocahontas then helped convince her tribe to let the English live.

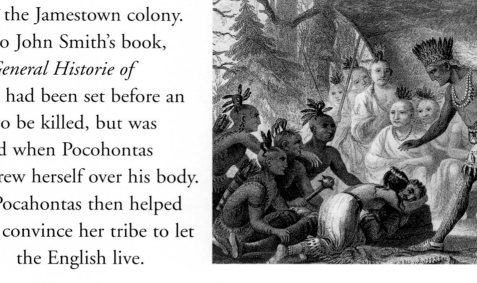

Pocahontas was both beautiful and intelligent, and she went on to help educate the English in the ways of the Indians. She also made her own people understand that the English were peaceful people, who did not want to fight the Indians.

In 1614, with Powhatan's approval, Pocahontas married the Englishman John Rolfe, a successful tobacco farmer. The marriage led to a time of peace between the Indians and the white settlers, which lasted until Powhatan's death. Pocahontas, now Lady Rebecca Rolfe, became a Christian, and eventually travelled to England, where she died.

21

Pontiac

The Ottawa Indian chief Pontiac (1720–69) organized a large resistance – known as 'Pontiac's War' – against the British invasion of Indian lands in the Great Lakes region of North America. His careful planning and dynamic style of command proved a dangerous challenge to the British. Pontiac became known as a strong leader and earned great respect from his own people and his opponents.

Pontiac was born in the Ohio territory and by 1755 he was a tribal chief. During the French and Indian War of 1760, Pontiac had agreed to let British troops pass through Indian land on their way to forts in the Michigan territory. Later, however, he began to fear that the Europeans would take over his people's hunting grounds and ancestral lands. To prevent this, he planned an attack on

the British forts and rallied support from Indian tribes from Lake Superior to the lower Mississippi. In May 1763, Pontiac ordered each tribe to attack the nearest fort.

Pontiac himself tried to capture the fort at Detroit, laying siege to it. Although his attack there failed, the other Indian forces were more successful. Eight of 12 posts were captured and many of the settlements and garrisons were destroyed. A peace treaty was signed between Pontiac and the British in July 1766, and for a short time there was peace between the chief and his former enemies. In 1769 Pontiac was visiting Illinois, when he was stabbed and killed by a Peoria Indian. A bitter war among the tribes resulted.

Joseph Brant and Little Turtle

Joseph Brant (1742–1807), called 'Thayendanegea' in his native tongue, was a Mohawk Indian chief. He became known for his great bravery during the American Revolution, when he fought for the British. The son of a Mohawk chief, he became a Christian and worked as an interpreter and translator for missionaries. Through his work, Brant became a great ambassador for both the Mohawks and the British. He was eventually made a captain in the British army, and visited England , to great honour.

Brant led his people in the Battle of Oriskany in 1777 and in the Cherry Valley

Massacre of 1778, as well as in many other campaigns during the American Revolution. Even when the British lost the war, Brant remained loyal to them. He made sure that the British and the Indians lived on peaceful terms with each other and made the British give the Mohawks money and land in payment for their help in the war.

Little Turtle (1751–1812) was a great Miami Indian chief, who helped to protect his tribe's native land in the Lake Michigan region from US invasion. He later led his people against General Anthony Wayne at the Battle of Fallen Timbers in 1794, but was eventually defeated by the Americans and deserted by the British, who had been helping him. From that time on, he spread the word that peace was the only way forward. While signing the Treaty of Greenville in August 1795, he said: 'I am the last to sign it, and I will be the last to break it.'

Tecumseh

Tecumseh (1768–1813) was a Shawnee warrior chief who, with his brother, the Shawnee Prophet, tried to stop the white colonists from settling in the Old Northwest. Tecumseh believed that Indians should be allowed to live their lives as they had before the settlers arrived. He argued that all Indians should stop the fighting between tribes, join together, and agree not to sell any of their lands to the settlers.

In 1809, tribes in the Indian Territory gave up a great deal of their land to the United States. Tecumseh, who was a great public speaker, went in person to the American President William Harrison, and explained that the land belonged to all Indians, and that one tribe did not have the right to sell it. Harrison ignored Tecumseh.

In the autumn of 1811, he decided to carry his message to the Chickasaw, Choctaw, and Creek tribes. He went south, leaving his brother in charge at 'Prophet's Town', a village he had set up for Indians to try to live their lives as they had before the Europeans arrived. Before he left, Tecumseh warned his brother not to attack Harrison's forces, which were nearby, but the Prophet ignored the warning. In the battle that followed, many Indians were killed and Prophet's Town was destroyed.

When Tecumseh returned, he joined the British against the Americans in the War of 1812. He was killed in the Battle of the Thames in Canada.

Black Hawk

The Black Hawk War in 1832 was the last major battle between the Indians and the white settlers, east of the Mississippi River. In 1804, the Sauk and Fox tribes had signed a treaty giving up all their land in Illinois. The Indians were supposed to resettle in Iowa, but many decided to remain east of the Mississippi until their lands were sold.

The Sauk leader, Black Hawk (1767–1838), did not want to give up his native land, and he fought against the treaty. When the Indians were finally ordered into Iowa in 1828, Black Hawk tried to join the Winnebago,

Potawatomi, and Kickapoo tribes together so they could fight for their lost land. In 1829, 1830 and 1831, Black Hawk's band returned across the Mississippi into their old land for the spring planting. They terrorized the white people who now lived there. When the Indians returned in 1832, an army was ready to stop them.

For 15 weeks this army chased Black Hawk back towards the Mississippi. The other tribes, which were supposed to help him fight the white people, did not give him any support. In fact, some of them even helped the army to track him down.

On 3 August 1832, what was left of Black Hawk's band was attacked as they tried to flee across the river. Almost all of them were killed. Black Hawk escaped but soon surrendered. He was sent to prison, but was later released and allowed to settle in a Sauk village on the Des Moines River.

Osceola

The leader of the Seminole Indians, in the second of the three 'Seminole Wars' between the Indians and the settlers, was Osceola (1804–38).

In 1832, some Seminole chiefs signed a treaty that called for them to move from their land in Florida to Indian Territory in present-day Oklahoma. Osceola and other young Seminoles were against the move and there was disagreement between the Indians. In 1835, a council was called at Fort Gibson to try and reach a new agreement. Osceola rose and plunged his dagger through the new treaty, saying 'this is the only treaty I will make with the whites!'. He was imprisoned, but was later released after he pretended to agree to the move.

In December 1835, the fighting began. Osceola knew that the Indians were no match for the white soldiers in open battle, so he led the Seminoles deep into the Everglades. From there he led the Indian braves in fierce raids on the white soldiers and settlers. General T. S. Jesup was eventually given an army of 8,000 US soldiers to fight the Seminoles and end the war.

In June 1837, Osceola and 200 warriors released the many Indians who were being held hostage by the Army, and this angered the government. General Jesup tricked Osceola by calling a truce and inviting him to peace talks. When Osceola arrived, he was seized and imprisoned. The great Indian warrior died in Fort Moultrie in Charleston, South Carolina, in 1838.

Crazy Horse and the Battle of Little Bighorn

The Indian chief Crazy Horse was one of the greatest warriors of the Sioux Indians. When the US government forced the Sioux to settle on the Pine Ridge reservation, Crazy Horse and another Sioux leader, Sitting Bull, refused to stay on the reservation and the tribe hunted freely in the surrounding area, fighting with their old enemies, the Crow and Blackfoot tribes, as well as with the white people.

When all the Sioux were ordered back to the reservation in December 1875, Crazy Horse challenged General George Crook to battle. This caused a series of conflicts, including the famous Battle of the Little Bighorn on 25 June 1876. This battle is also known as 'Custer's Last Stand'.

Sitting Bull and Crazy Horse were preparing their tribe for battle, so the US Army sent a few soldiers to try to calm the Indians down. On 24 June, Colonel George Armstrong Custer and his troops found the Sioux camp on the Little Bighorn River in Montana. Custer did not realize how large the Indian forces were and he attacked them with only a small army of about 225 men. In the battle, Custer and all his men were killed.

After this, the government sent in many more troops to suppress the Sioux and after a hard winter, Crazy Horse was persuaded to surrender by his uncle Spotted Tail. Even in defeat, Crazy Horse was brave and proud. He and his band of warriors entered Fort Robinson dressed in their finest war regalia to give themselves up. Crazy Horse was imprisoned, and while struggling to escape, he was stabbed in the back and killed.

Sitting Bull and the Wounded Knee Massacre

Sitting Bull, or 'Tatanka Iyotake' (1831–90), was a great Sioux leader, who is best known for his help in defeating General Custer at Little Bighorn.

When he was just a teenager, Sitting Bull fought enemy tribes and white people who invaded the Sioux lands. He was the best at all the things most admired by the Sioux Indians: he was brave, wise, determined and generous. He refused to let the whites have the land in the Black Hills after gold was discovered there in the mid-1870s, because this was sacred ground for his tribe.

The Wounded Knee massacre, which occurred on 28 December 1890 at Wounded Knee Creek in the Pine Ridge Sioux Reservation, was the last major clash between US troops and American Indians. The main cause of the battle was the Sioux's new 'Ghost Dance' religion, which was based on the idea that the Indians should be allowed to live their lives in freedom, as they had before the white people invaded.

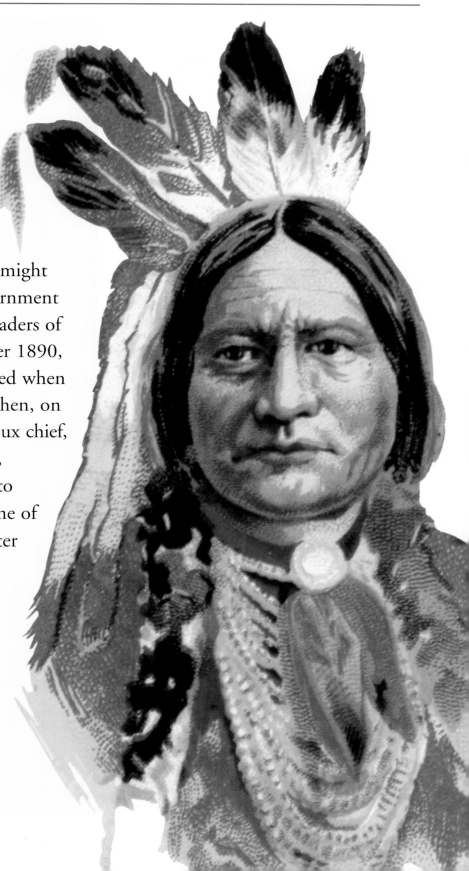

Worried that the Sioux's new religion might cause a rebellion, the government sent troops to arrest the leaders of the tribe. On 15 December 1890, Chief Sitting Bull was killed when they tried to arrest him. Then, on 28 December, another Sioux chief, Big Foot, and his followers, were caught and brought to Wounded Knee Creek. One of the Indians fired a shot after they were ordered to put down their weapons, and the US troops fired back, killing Chief Big Foot and many others. Some who survived the first shots were chased and killed, including many women and children.

Chief Joseph

Chief Joseph (1840–1904) was a leader of the Nez Perce Indian tribe. The Nez Perce had always been friendly with the white people, and had once occupied much territory in the region where Washington, Oregon, and Idaho now join.

When they signed the Stevens Treaty of 1855, the Nez Perce agreed to give up most of their land to the US government in return for a large reservation in Oregon and Idaho. When gold was discovered in Oregon in 1863, however, the government demanded that the Nez Perce give up this part of the reservation, too.

Chief Joseph resisted, but later agreed to move peacefully with his people to the Lapwai Reservation in Idaho.

Fighting broke out in 1877 when young Nez Perce warriors decided to take revenge on the white settlers for forcing the tribe off their land. There were many more US soldiers than Nez Perce Indians, but Chief Joseph and his tribe still managed to defeat them. He then led his people on a retreat of more than a thousand miles in an effort to reach Canada, where the white settlers and the Indians lived more peacefully together.

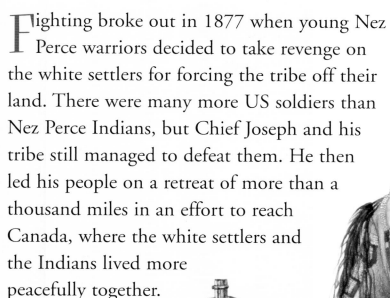

On 30 September 1877, US troops overtook the Nez Perce a short way from the Canadian border. Because most of his warriors were dead or wounded and his people were starving, Chief Joseph surrendered, saying 'I will fight no more forever'. Sent to Indian Territory in Oklahoma, the Nez Perce were allowed to return to Idaho in 1883.

Geronimo

The name 'Geronimo' is a Spanish nickname for Jerome. The great Indian chief Geronimo's real name was Goyathlay, which means 'one who yawns'. Geronimo was a medicine man and prophet of the Chiricahua Apaches, who fought against both the white invaders and the authorities. In 1874, the government decided that the Chiricahua, like many other Indian tribes, should be moved from their native lands in Arizona to a reservation. Geronimo and other young members of the tribe fled to Mexico to escape. After a time, however, Geronimo returned to his tribe's ancient lands to cultivate the land and continue their way of life.

In 1882, Geronimo led a group of Chiricahua Indians against the forces of US General George J. Crook, and a series of battles followed until 1885, as Geronimo fought against further colonization of the Indian lands. He became known as a great leader and warrior.

In 1886, determined to stop the Indians once and for all, Crook sent out a large army of soldiers which was instructed to capture or destroy Geronimo and his followers. Geronimo and 340 others were captured and sent as prisoners to Florida, then Alabama, and, finally, Oklahoma. The government promised that the Chiricahua could eventually return to Arizona, but this promise was not kept. Instead, Geronimo and his people were put to hard labour, far from their families.

Other Great Chiefs

Cornplanter (*c*.1735–1836) was a famous Seneca Indian chief. He was the son of an Indian woman who had married a white settler, so he was part Seneca and part European. During the American Revolution, Cornplanter led his warriors against the colonists in several important campaigns. When Cornplanter realized that the British had lost, he became a loyal supporter of the United States in an effort to maintain peaceful relations between the Indians and the white people.

Red Jacket (*c*.1758–1830), also known as Sagoyewatha, was a fiery Seneca chief. He worked secretly with both the Indians and the whites to make sure that he was well thought of by both. After the Seneca tribe was persuaded by the British to join the American Revolution, Red Jacket proved to be an unenthusiastic warrior, although he wore the British uniform coat, which earned him his English name 'Red Jacket'. After the war, he tried to keep the peace between his people and the United States.

William Weatherford, also known as 'Red Eagle' (1780–1824), was a Creek Indian chief who is best remembered for his role in the Creek War, 1812–14. Red Eagle led 1,000 Creek Indians in an attack on US troops in Fort Mims, Alabama. Nearly 500 soldiers and settlers were killed. Red Eagle then led his forces to Horseshoe Bend, where they fought a bitter battle against President Andrew Jackson and a group of Indians who had agreed to help him. Six hundred of Red Eagle's warriors were killed, and the Creek Indians lost about half of their land in Alabama. Jackson admired Red Eagle's skill and courage, and instead of taking him prisoner, he let him go.

41

Spotted Tail, or 'Sinte Gleska' (1826–1881), was a leader of the Brule Sioux, and was famous for standing up for the customs, land and rights of his people. In 1866, Spotted Tail went to peace talks at Fort Laramie, but despite his efforts, the Sioux lost most of their land. After gold was discovered in the sacred Black Hills, Spotted Tail tried to persuade the Americans not to send the Dakotas, who lived in the Hills, to a reservation. Although he did not succeed, Spotted Tail had impressed the government, and it named him head chief of the Brule band and made him a lieutenant in the US Army.

Cochise, chief of the central Chiricahua tribe, was one of the most famous Apache leaders to protect his land from white settlers during the nineteeth century. In 1861, Cochise and several of his relatives were accused of kidnapping a white child, and were held prisoner in a US army camp. Cochise managed to escape by cutting a hole in a tent, but the other Apache hostages were hanged. Cochise joined forces with Mangas Coloradas, the leader of another Chiricahua band, and took his revenge by attacking white settlements. He surrendered in 1871 and died in 1874 on the new Chiricahua reservation, which was built on land that had been owned by his people for hundreds of years.

Places to Visit and Things to Do

British Museum – Great Russell Street, London, WC1B 3DG. Telephone: 0171 636 1555.

Horniman Museum – 100 London Road, Forest Hill, London, SE23 3PQ. Telephone: 0181 699 1872.

The Livesey Museum – 682 Old Kent Road, London, SE15 1JF. Telephone: 0171 639 5604

The Natural History Museum – Cromwell Road, London, SW7 5BD. Telephone: 0171 938 9123.

Further Reading

Eyewitness Guides: North America Indian, Dorling Kindersley in association with The American Museum of Natural History, 1995.

History of the World: Civilization of America, Cherrytree Books, 1990.

Make It Work: North American Indians, Two-Can, 1995.

Native Americans, Wayland, 1992.

Plains Indians, by Fiona MacDonald, Oxford University Press, 1992.

Videos and CD Roms

DK Children's Encyclopedia, Dorling Kindersley
History of the World, Dorling Kindersley (CD Rom)
Pocahontas, Walt Disney Video
The Wild West, Channel 4 Video Series

Picture Credits

Bridgeman Art Library:
pp. 11, 12, 14,
16, 17, 24, 31, 34(l)
Christie's Images: pp. 13,
22-23
**Mary Evans Picture
Library:** pp. 8, 19, 21, 26,
27, 28, 29, 30, 33, 34(r),
35, 36, 38, 40, 42, 43
**Gravesend Tourist Information
Centre:** pp. 20, 20-21
Salamander Picture Library:
pp. 10, 25, 37, 39
Visual Arts Library: pp. 15, 18,
32, 41, 44